SCIENCE WIDE OPEN

Women in Biology

Written by Mary Wissinger
Illustrated by Danielle Pioli

Created and edited by John J. Coveyou

Science, Naturally!
An imprint of Platypus Media, LLC
Washington, D.C.

What makes a butterfly?

A caterpillar grows into a butterfly, but nobody knew exactly how that change, which is called metamorphosis, happened...

...until Maria Sibylla Merian.

She loved insects so much that she spent years watching and drawing them. She travelled across the ocean to study the life cycles of caterpillars and other bugs.

(Germany, 1647–1717)

Maria's drawings were very detailed and beautiful, and they gave scientists important information about insects and plants.

Her drawings were used in the Linnaean system that organizes all living things. This system is important in all of biology.

Hang on. What is biology?

Well, if we compared you and a rock, we'd find a lot of differences. But the biggest one is that you're alive, and a rock isn't. Biology looks at everything that is alive, like plants, animals, and you! People have been studying life for a long time.

Almost a thousand years ago, Hildegard of Bingen wrote about biology and medicine. Back then, people didn't understand that they could get sick from drinking dirty water.

Hildegard figured out that water should be cleaned first, and this stopped people from getting sick. She also studied how plants could be used as medicines, and shared her ideas so people could have better health.

(Germany, 1098–1179)

13

So...
biology keeps me from getting sick?

It can, because biology teaches us all about how the body works.

When we know what makes us sick, then we can find ways to get better.

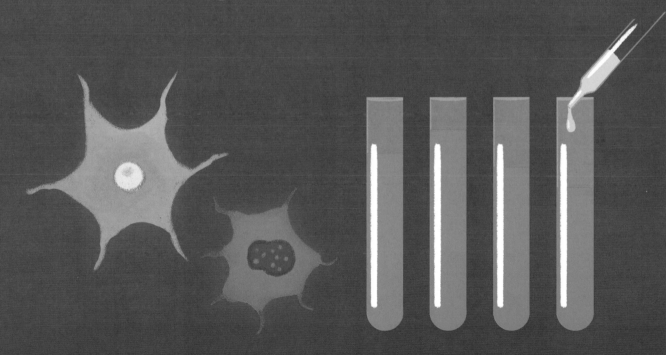

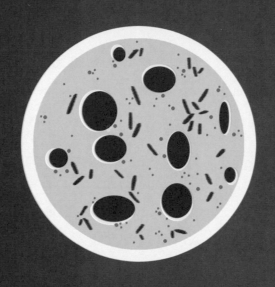

Just look at Jane Cooke Wright!

She was a doctor who saved many lives by running experiments in her laboratory. She grew cells in petri dishes and then watched what different medicines did to the cells. Her observations helped her pick the best treatments to give her patients.

(United States, 1919–2013)

17

What are cells?

All living things are made of cells—
your body is made up of trillions!

Each cell has its own special job. Muscle cells help
you move, and skin cells protect your body.

The cells inside your nose help you smell.

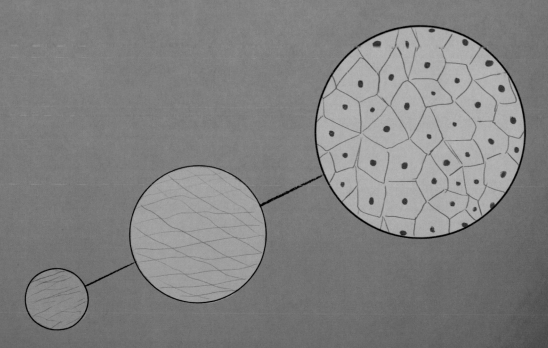

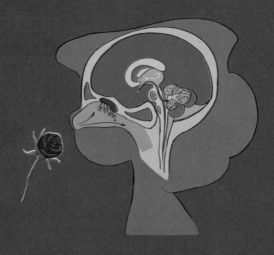

Linda Buck won a Nobel Prize because she helped discover that nose cells have tiny message receivers called receptors.

When different smells hit the receptors, the cells send messages to your brain.

That's why, even if you closed your eyes, you could smell the difference between a flower and a dog.

21

(United States, 1947–)

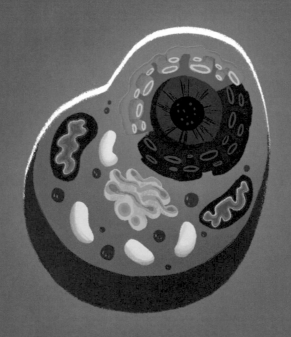

Wow. But how does a cell know its special job?

Inside of every cell is an instruction manual called DNA.

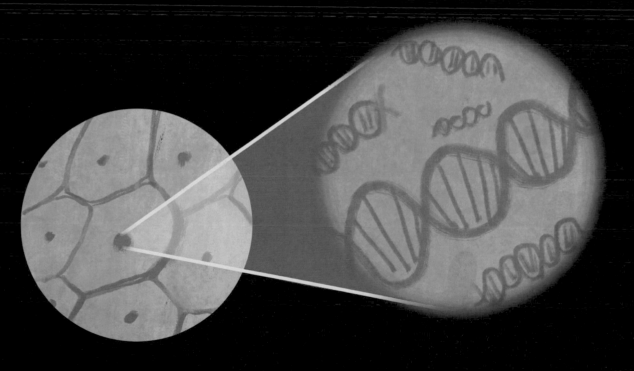

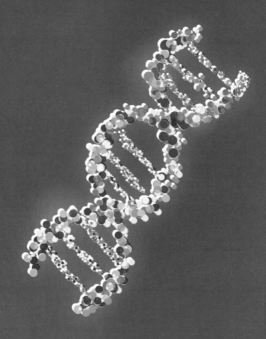

It's the blueprint, or plan, for your whole body. DNA tells the body how to make cells and build body parts like muscles, bones, and skin. It also determines the color of your eyes and hair, and is what makes you *you.*

But DNA is not just in people's cells. It's also found in all living things.

Barbara McClintock studied DNA in corn, and discovered something completely amazing. By observing the colors in corn kernels, she learned that parts of DNA—genes—can actually switch places!

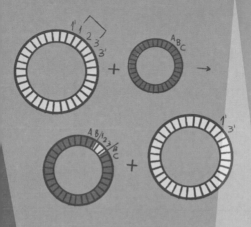

Chromosomes

Jumping Genes

27

(United States, 1902–1992)

She named these jumping genes transposons.

Transposons were such a surprise that it was many years before people realized she was right and awarded her a Nobel Prize.

Barbara loved figuring out tricky problems. When she made a hypothesis—or scientific guess—she worked hard on her research and experiments to find answers.

And it's a good thing, because her work with DNA and transposons taught us so much about our genes and DNA.

You can start researching right now. Pick something that you like and ask a question.

Ok! Why do butterflies have different colors?

Go on and take your own guess—that's your hypothesis.

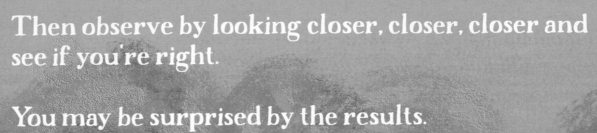

Then observe by looking closer, closer, closer and see if you're right.

You may be surprised by the results.

Can you find...?

Maria Sibylla Merian *(muh-REE-uh see-BAY-la MAH-ri-ohn)*

Hildegard of Bingen *(HILL-dih-gard of BING-en)*

Linda Buck *(LIN-duh BUCK)*

Barbara McClintock *(BAR-bruh muh-CLIN-tock)*

Jane Cooke Wright *(JANE COOK RITE)*

Glossary

BIOLOGY: The scientific study of living things.

CELLS: Small compartments that hold the biological equipment that keeps an organism alive and working. Cells are the basic structural unit for all organisms.

DNA (Deoxyribonucleic Acid): The written plan in the cells of living things (like plants, animals, and people) which tells each cell, and as a consequence, the body, how to grow and function.

EXPERIMENT: A test to collect information about the world to see if a hypothesis is correct.

GENES: Smaller sections of DNA that contribute to how specific parts of living things (like the color of corn, or our hair and eyes) will look and grow.

HYPOTHESIS: A scientific guess that a scientist makes to explain something they think is true or they think will happen.

LINNAEAN SYSTEM: A way to organize all living things into groups based on traits that living things have in common.

METAMORPHOSIS: The change that happens to a caterpillar when it becomes a butterfly.

NOBEL PRIZE: An award given for amazing work in chemistry, physics, physiology, medicine, literature, or economics. Being given a Nobel Prize is one of the greatest honors a scientist can get!

OBSERVATION: Using our senses to collect information about the world around us.

RECEPTOR: A small part of a cell that allows the cell to sense and respond to things around it.

RESEARCH: To investigate and study something to learn new things about it.

TRANSPOSONS (Jumping Genes): Genes that can switch places with other genes in a DNA strand.

Bibliography

Hypatia's Heritage: A History of Women in Science from Antiquity through the Nineteenth Century by Margaret Alic (Beacon Press, 1986).

Magnificent Minds: 16 Pioneering Women in Science & Medicine by Pendred E. Noyce (Tumblehome Learning, Inc., 2015).

Notable Women Scientists edited by Pamela Proffitt. (Gale Group, 1999).

Remarkable Minds: 17 More Pioneering Women in Science & Medicine by Pendred E. Noyce (Tumblehome Learning, Inc., 2015).

Science Wide Open: Women in Biology
Copyright © 2020, 2019, 2016 Genius Games, LLC
Originally published by Genius Games, LLC in 2016

Written by Mary Wissinger
Illustrated by Danielle Pioli
Created and edited by John J. Coveyou

Published by Science, Naturally!
English hardback first edition • 2016 • ISBN: 978-1-945779-09-1
    Second edition • November 2019
English paperback first edition • October 2020 • ISBN: 978-1-938492-30-3
English eBook first edition • 2016 • ISBN: 978-1-945779-12-1
    Second edition • November 2019
Spanish paperback first edition • October 2020 • ISBN: 978-1-938492-07-5
Spanish eBook first edition • October 2020 • ISBN: 978-1-938492-29-7

Enjoy all the titles in the series:
    Women in Biology • Las mujeres en la biología
    Women in Chemistry • Las mujeres en la química
    Women in Physics • Las mujeres en la física
        More titles coming soon!

Teacher's Guide available at the Educational Resources page of ScienceNaturally.com.

Published in the United States by:
    Science, Naturally!
        An imprint of Platypus Media, LLC
    725 8th Street, SE, Washington, D.C. 20003
    202-465-4798 • Fax: 202-558-2132
    Info@ScienceNaturally.com • ScienceNaturally.com

Distributed to the trade by:
    National Book Network (North America)
        301-459-3366 • Toll-free: 800-462-6420
        CustomerCare@NBNbooks.com • NBNbooks.com
    NBN international (worldwide)
        NBNi.Cservs@IngramContent.com • Distribution.NBNi.co.uk

Library of Congress Control Number: 2020016422

10 9 8 7 6 5 4 3 2 1

Printed in Canada